Mac's Big Wish

Big and Best Wishes!

Ruth Vanderwall *Laura Lillian*

I am not Paul Thiessen

Mac's Big Wish

written by
Peter Vanderwall

Illustrated by
Janis Lillian

Sophie & Sheba Books
LUMINARE PRESS

Mac's Big Wish
Text copyright © 2022 Peter Vanderwall
Illustrations copyright © 2022 Janis Lillian
All rights reserved.

This book or any portion thereof may not be
reproduced or used in any manner whatsoever without the
express written permission of the publisher, except for the use
of brief quotations in a book review. No illustration may be
reproduced or used in any manner whatsoever without
the express written permission of the publisher.

Printed in the United States of America

Written by Peter Vanderwall
Illustrated by Janis Lillian
Project Coordinated by Kathleen Heide Vanderwall

Luminare Press
442 Charnelton Street
Eugene, OR 97401
www.luminarepress.com

LCCN: 2021925580
ISBN: 978-1-64388-388-5

For Sophie, Sandy, and Perky,
my best friends in life.

—P.V.

To all my furry friends,
thanks for your unconditional love.

—J.L.

"Mac, you sure are a cuddly puppy," said Mr. Puddleton as he put the little dog in the front window of Puddleton's Pet Rescue.

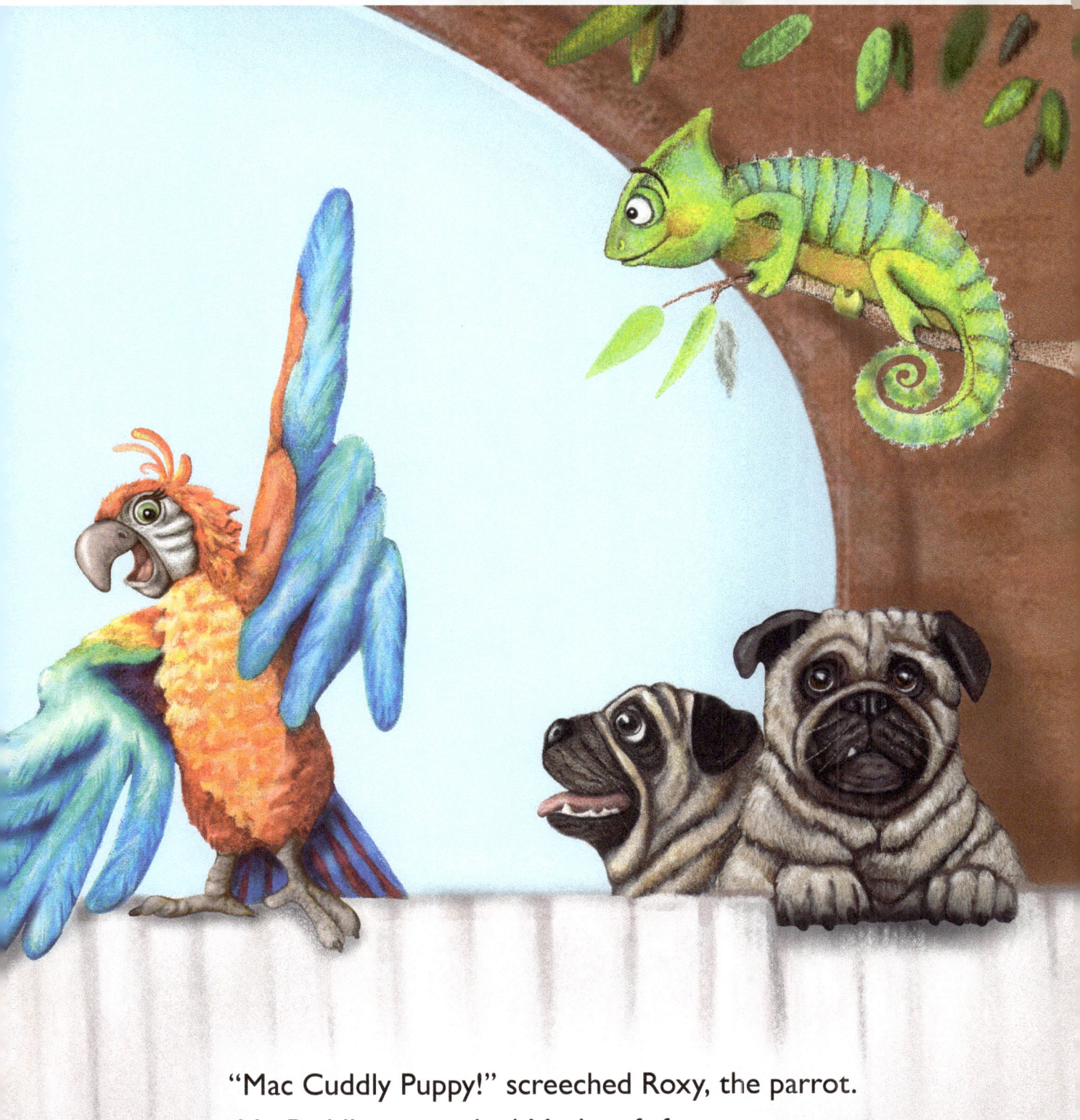

"Mac Cuddly Puppy!" screeched Roxy, the parrot. Mr. Puddleton stroked Mac's soft fur. "You're so snuggly, someone will probably take you home today."

Just then, with a *squish-squash-squish*, a man clomped into the shop. He took a quick look at Mac, then *squish-squash-squished* straight to Sandy, the yellow Labrador.

"Just the dog I've been looking for!" he exclaimed. "You're going to be the best retriever ever."

Mac watched Sandy scamper away.

Outside the shop, everyone rushed about, except for one small woman.
Her face looked sad, until she spotted Mac and stepped inside.

"What's your name, little puppy?"
"Mac Cuddly Puppy!" Roxy squawked.
"I'm pleased to meet you, Mac.
My name is Emma."

Emma rubbed Mac's belly, fluffed his fur, and tickled his ears.

Mac nuzzled Emma's hands, snuggled her cheek, and sniffed her hair.

"I wish I could take you home with me, Mac," said Emma.

That evening, Mr. Puddleton turned off the lights and locked the door.
He called out, "Good night, everybody!"
"Good night, everybody!" Roxy mimicked.

Mac curled up in his bed and gazed out into the night.
The full moon looked alone in the dark sky.

"Mac Cuddly Puppy!" screeched Roxy at sunrise.

"That's right, Roxy," Mr. Puddleton agreed. "I bet somebody takes Mac home today."

Soon, with a *click-clack, click-clack,* a woman walked into the shop.

She *click-clack, click-clacked* straight to Precious, the poodle. "Just the dog I've been looking for! You're going to win first prize at all the shows!"

Mac watched Precious prance away.

That afternoon, Emma returned to the shop.
"I thought somebody would have
taken you home by now, Mac."
She smiled as she stroked Mac's fluffy fur.
"I wish I could take you home with me."

Mac wished so, too.

Roxy woke Mac up the next morning with her screeching. "Mac Cuddly Puppy!" "Surely someone will take you home today, Mac," Mr. Puddleton said.

Moments later, a couple raced into the shop, their running shoes *squeak-squeak-squeaking*. They glanced at Mac and then jogged straight to Dash, the greyhound.

"Just the dog we've been looking for!" they cheered.

"You're going to be the fastest dog at the park!"

Mac watched Dash dart away.

Just then, Emma limped into the shop. She winced with each step, but her face softened with a smile and her eyes sparkled as she petted Mac.

"I wish I could take you home with me."
Mac wished she could, too.

One morning Mr. Puddleton
put a new puppy in Mac's spot
and carried Mac back to a pen by the turtles.
"Maybe this is your lucky spot, Mac."

But Mac wondered
if he would *ever* be just the
right dog for anyone.

He couldn't retrieve like Sandy
or prance like Precious
or run like Dash.

He was just Mac.
He didn't feel special at all.

Mac sighed.
At least Emma would visit and snuggle him.
Mac waited all day, but Emma didn't come in.

Days passed and still, no Emma.
Days turned to weeks and still, no Emma.

Then one morning, a woman *pad-pad-padded* into the shop. Her name tag read, "Virginia."

"I'm looking for a special dog. For a special job."

"There are some nice puppies in the window," Mr. Puddleton offered.

Virginia shook her head. "No."

"Perhaps one of these?" Mr. Puddleton pointed to a pen of pugs.

"No, they won't do either." Virginia frowned and *pad-pad-padded* toward the door. "I guess I'll try somewhere else."

Suddenly Roxy squawked, "Mac Cuddly Puppy!"

"Mac? Cuddly? Puppy?" Virginia laughed.
"He's here in the back,"
said Mr. Puddleton, leading the way.
When Mac saw Virginia,
he wiggled all over and wagged his nubby tail.

"Mac, you're just the dog I've been looking for!" Virginia smiled wide.
"You're going to be the best dog for a special job!"

Mr. Puddleton smiled and Roxy flapped her wings as they watched Mac ride away with Virginia.

Mac followed Virginia into a big room.

"Ladies and gentlemen,
 I'd like you to meet a new friend,"
Virginia announced. "His name is..."

Then a familiar voice cried out.

"Mac!"

"I'm so happy you're here!"
Emma beamed.
"My wish came true!"

Mac wiggled in delight.
His wish had come true, too.

It wasn't long before Mac made friends with everyone.

He exercised with Ed.

And sang a song with Sally.

He watched a Western with Wyatt.

And gardened with Grace.

That evening Mac settled into his new bed
at the end of the hallway. It was warm and cozy.

He looked out the window at the night sky.
The moon was only a sliver, but it didn't look lonely anymore.
Thousands of stars twinkled around it.

A familiar hand softly petted Mac's back.
Emma was looking up at the night sky, too.
"It's a big universe, Mac.
And you're a part of it."
Her eyes twinkled like the stars.
"Good night, my friend."

Mac closed his eyes and drifted off to sleep.

He wasn't a good retriever like Sandy.

Or a prize-winner like Precious.

Or a fast runner like Dash.

He was Mac.
He had the best job of all.
He was a good friend.

How lucky can a dog get?

Photograph by Kathleen Heide Vanderwall

Peter Vanderwall was inspired to write *Mac's Big Wish* by a bedtime story that he told his sons, Eric and Kenny, when they were growing up. He is also a screenwriter whose produced movies include *Hide Away*, *Reverse Angle*, and *Shadowheart*. Peter lives with his wife, Kathleen, in the Pacific Northwest where they enjoy skiing, hiking, biking, and other outdoor adventures.

Visit the author's website at **petervanderwall.com**.

Sign up for our email list to learn more about the *Mac's Big Wish* series and therapy dogs' contributions as friends and companions.

Special thanks to the Burleigh family, the Capostagno-Shepherd family, the Gambino family, the Gentile family, the Heide families, the Inman family, the Strickland family, BJ Toewe, and Amy Betz of Tiny Tales Editing for their valuable help and suggestions. Tremendous thanks to Sophie, our dog, who is with Peter in the photo above. Sophie was our best friend and beloved companion through many times, happy and sad.

Janis Lillian is an illustrator whose art and innovations have been put to use by the likes of Crayola, Hallmark, Kelly's Crafts and Freckle Press. Her whimsical designs and lovable characters come to life in pen and ink detail and watercolor-soaked splendor. A self-taught artist with an abundant curiosity about art and life, Janis lives in a happy state of chaos among family and friends in the Pacific Northwest.

Photograph by Stacey Griffin

Kathleen Heide Vanderwall, the author's soul mate, coordinated the making of *Mac's Big Wish*. Growing up in eastern Oregon, Kathleen's best friend was Sheba, an Arabian mare. Kathleen and Sheba rode many trails and competed in barrel races at local rodeos. In addition to this book, she has coordinated other projects including those about fossils, medicine, oceans, and education.

Photograph by Peter Vanderwall

Printed in the USA
CPSIA information can be obtained
at www.ICGtesting.com
JSHW040609311023
51154JS00004B/8